MAGIC SHOW

VIRGINIA LOH-HAGAN

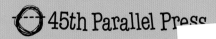
45th Parallel Press

Published in the United States of America by
Ann Arbor, Michigan
www.cherrylakepublishing.com

Reading Adviser: Marla Conn, ReadAbility, In
Book Designer: Felicia Macheske

Photo Credits: © Eric Isselee/Shutterstock.com, cover, 1; © serg_dibrova /Shutterstock.com, 3; © Mr.Boy/Shutterstock.com, 5; © Martina_L/Shutterstock.com, 7; © shank_ali/iStock, 9; © Peter Baxter/Shutterstock.com, 10; © Julian Rovagnati/Shutterstock.com, 11; © MAEWJPHO/Shutterstock.com, 14; © Ljupco/Thinkstock, 17, 31; © Elnur/Sv, 18; © Dmytro Zinkevych/Shutterstock.com, 20; © carebott/iStock/Getty, 21; © Jupiterimages/Thinkstock, 23; © View Stock/Thinkstock, 27; © Steve Debenport/iStock, 29; © Carbonell/Shutterstock.com, 30; © catalin eremia/Shutterstock.com, 31; © wavebreakmedia/Shutterstock.com, back cover; © Dora Zett/Shutterstock.com, back cover

Graphics Elements: © pashabo/Shutterstock.com, 6, back cover; © axako/Shutterstock.com, 7; © Art'nLera/Shutterstock.com, 7, back cover; © IreneArt/Shutterstock.com, 4, 8; © bokasin/Shutterstock.com, 11, 19; © Belausava Volha/Shutterstock.com, 12, 20; © Nik Merkulov/Shutterstock.com, 13; © Ya Tshey/Shutterstock.com, 16, 25; © kubais/Shutterstock.com, 17; © Sasha Nazim/Shutterstock.com, 15, 22; © Ursa Major/Shutterstock.com, 26, 29; © Infomages/Shutterstock.com, 24; © topform/Shutterstock.com, 25, back cover

45th Parallel Press is an imprint of Cherry Lake Publishing.

Library of Congress Cataloging-in-Publication Data

Loh-Hagan, Virginia.
  Magic show / by Virginia Loh-Hagan.
      pages cm. — (D.I.Y. make it happen)
  Includes bibliographical references and index.
  ISBN 978-1-63470-493-9 (hardcover) — ISBN 978-1-63470-553-0 (pdf) — ISBN 978-1-63470-613-1 (pbk.) — ISBN 978-1-63470-673-5 (ebook)
  1. Magic shows—Juvenile literature. 2. Magic tricks—Juvenile literature. I. Title.
  GV1548.L55 2016
  793.8—dc23
                              2015026837

Cherry Lake Publishing would like to acknowledge the work of The Partnership for 21st Century Skills.
Please visit *www.p21.org* for more information.

Printed in the United States of America
Corporate Graphics Inc.

ABOUT THE AUTHOR

Dr. Virginia Loh-Hagan is an author, university professor, former classroom teacher, and curriculum designer. She believes in magic. She also believes in dragons. She lives in San Diego with her very tall husband and very naughty dogs. To learn more about her, visit www.virginialoh.com.

TABLE OF CONTENTS

CHAPTER ONE

WHAT DOES IT MEAN TO PUT ON A MAGIC SHOW?

Do you love magic? Do you love performing? Do you love creating tricks? Then putting on a magic show is the right project for you!

Magicians practice **stage magic**. Stage magic is the art of entertaining. Magicians perform **illusions**. Illusions are magic tricks. It's when you get people to believe things. People believe magicians do impossible things. Magicians amaze people. They trick people.

They put on magic shows. They show off their tricks. Tricks are also called **effects**.

An example is pulling a rabbit from a hat. Another example is making something disappear. They perform for an **audience**. Audience refers to people who watch a show.

Go to magic shows. Talk to other magicians.

KNOW THE LINGO

Abracadabra: magic word to help magicians make something happen

Bad angle: people sitting at certain positions that allow them to see how a magic trick is done

Cardician: a magician who does only card tricks

Crimp: bending a part of a card in order to use it

Daub: wax used to make things stick

Fakir: a performer who does crazy stunts like walking on fire or charming snakes

Flash paper: special paper that burns in a bright flash

Hat production: the act of producing objects from hats

Hocus-pocus: magic word to help magicians make something happen

Load: secretly putting an object somewhere

Prestidigitation: performed with quick fingers

Presto: magic word for "quickly"

Profonde: large pocket in a suit that allows magicians to make items disappear by tossing them into the pocket

Voila: word for "here it is"

Stage magic is different from magic. Magic refers to spells. It refers to witches and wizards. Magic is popular in fantasy stories. Stage magicians are not wizards. They're special actors. They have special skills.

Most magicians are performers. They like being onstage. They like doing tricks. They like challenges. They like solving puzzles.

You'll have fun putting on a magic show. You'll plan tricks. You'll create illusions. You'll wow your audiences. You might also make some money. Magicians perform. Then they get paid.

Ask magicians how much they make. They make different amounts of money.

CHAPTER TWO

WHAT DO YOU NEED TO PUT ON A MAGIC SHOW?

There are many types of magic shows. Learn about them. Decide what type you want to do.

➡ **Close-up magic shows are for a small crowd. The audience is close to you. Street magic is an example. You perform in the streets. People don't know they're getting a show. You collect tips. Tips are when people give you money.**

➡ **Party magic shows are for parties. Magic shows are most popular at kids' birthday parties. You perform. People pay you at the end.**

➡ **Stage illusions are big shows. You perform in a theater. You use big props. Props are objects. They help create effects. Audience members buy tickets.**

Consider doing magic shows online.
Have an adult help!

There are many types of magic tricks. Decide the tricks you want to do. All tricks can be learned.

➡ **Card** tricks use cards.

➡ **Production** tricks produce something from nothing. An example is pulling a coin from behind someone's ear.

➡ **Vanish** tricks make something disappear.

➡ **Escape** tricks mean you get out of something. An example is escaping from a locked cage.

- ➡ **Transformation** tricks change things. An example is changing a boy into a bird.

- ➡ **Restoration** tricks change things back.

- ➡ **Transportation** tricks move things.

- ➡ **Levitation** tricks make things float in the air.

- ➡ **Penetration** tricks make an object pass through another.

- ➡ **Mentalism** is when magicians read people's minds.

- ➡ **Prediction** tricks are when magicians predict the future.

Make sure you only share secrets with other magicians.

Put on your own show! Putting on a magic show is like planning an event.

➡ **Decide where you want to put on your magic show. Use places available to you. Some examples are your house, backyard, or school. You could perform in the streets. You could rent a space.**

➡ **Decide a time. Consider doing it over the weekend. Decide how many days or nights you want your show to run.**

➡ **Come up with a name. You want a magician name. You want a show name.**

➡ **Create business cards. Include your information.**

➡ **Create and send out invitations. Let people know about your show. Make posters. Use the Internet. Use e-mail.**

Get an adult to help you rent a space.

TRY THIS!

There's time between people coming and the show starting. Keep your audience members busy. Keep them engaged. Create activity stations.

You'll need: tables or blocked-off areas, posters of optical illusions, puzzles, timer, playing cards, game rules

Steps

1 Create a station of optical illusions. These are pictures. They trick the eyes. Provide 6 to 10 different optical illusions. Challenge people to figure out what they're seeing.

2 Create a station of puzzles. These puzzles shouldn't take a long time to finish. Include a timer. Tell people to finish the puzzles in three minutes or less.

3 Create a station of cards. Leave out several decks of cards. Challenge people to play quick card games. Think of three to four games. Examples are Slapjack and Go Fish. Include game rules.

You'll have to learn many tricks.

Get friends to help you.

➡ **Get an assistant. This person helps you with tricks. This person helps you set up.**

➡ **Get a stooge. A stooge pretends to be an audience member. A stooge is really a part of your act.**

Get supplies.

➡ **Get a costume. Some magicians wear a black hat. They wear a black cape. They wear white gloves. They have a wand.**

➡ **Get props. These are things needed for your tricks. Popular props are playing cards. You'll find most things at a store. You probably have a lot of things in your house. Reuse whenever possible.**

➡ **Consider buying magic trick kits. Check the Internet.**

➡ **Get a trunk. This is a big case. You need to carry your stuff.**

CHAPTER THREE

HOW DO YOU SET UP A MAGIC SHOW?

Set up your stage. Do this before the audience comes.

- ➡ Decide where your audience will sit. Set up chairs. Or put blankets on the ground. Make sure people are sitting in front of you.

- ➡ Decide where you'll perform. Create a stage area. People need to see you.

- ➡ Set up a table for props.

- ➡ Set up your props.

BILLY KIDD

Billy Kidd danced. She played musical instruments. She acted. She combined all her skills. She helped magicians with their moves onstage. She watched a street magician. It inspired her. She became one of the few female magicians. She's been on television. She puts on magic shows all over the world. She likes making audiences happy. She likes doing tricks. Her favorites are card tricks. She said, "My best advice for anyone in magic is to educate and indulge yourself in other art forms. Go and watch live theater, concerts, movies. Watch other people perform. Learn from other performers. Take classes in acting and dance and even music. And I don't mean a one-week course. Do it for years. Learn about yourself. Learn about all your bad habits. ... Learn to take constructive criticism. This will make you a stronger and more confident performer."

Be loud so people can hear you.

Consider setting up a snack table.

➡ **Sell snacks. Make popcorn. Put it in paper bags. Staple your business card to the bag.**

➡ **Sell drinks.**

➡ **Get someone to take care of this table.**

Practice tricks many times.

You can't have a magic show without tricks. Learn a bunch of them.

➡ **Read books.**

➡ **Read online articles.**

➡ **Watch online videos.**

Card tricks are the most popular magic tricks. There are tons of them. An example is making a card change into another card.

➡ **Place the trick card directly under the top card.**

➡ **Place your hand on top of the cards.**

➡ **Push the top card up a little.**

➡ **Use the bottom part of your palm. Pull back the trick card. Free it from the pack.**

➡ **Push the trick card forward in your hand.**

➡ **Slide the trick card over the pack. It becomes the new top card.**

Learn how to use your hands.
Make big gestures.

Card tricks rely on **sleight of hand**. This means tricking people using your hands. Sleights are hidden movements. The key to tricks is to **misdirect** people. Distract them. This means get them thinking about something else. There are different ways to misdirect people.

➡ **Make people look away. People will follow your eyes. So look at different things.**

➡ **Use big actions. They cover small actions. Your right hand is doing a trick. Do something crazy with your left hand.**

➡ **Use wands to direct people's attention. They'll follow the wand.**

➡ **Use patter. Patter is what you say during the show. You may tell stories. You may tell jokes.**

CHAPTER FOUR

HOW DO YOU RUN A MAGIC SHOW?

You've sent the invitations. You've set everything up. You're ready for the big show!

There are things to do before the show.

➡ Greet people as they come in.

➡ Have someone collect money or donations.

➡ Guide people to their seats.

➡ Have your assistant introduce you.

➡ Enter the stage. Bow to your audience.

Magic shows have three parts.

- ➡ **First is the opener. It's a fast and flashy trick. It catches the audience's attention.**

- ➡ **Second is the middle material. It's harder tricks. They're longer. They need more time to set up.**

- ➡ **Third is the closer. It's the best trick. The audience will remember this trick the most.**

Remember to bow after the show.

QUICK TIPS

- Practice in front of a mirror. See what your audience will see.

- Never do the same trick more than once for the same audience. You don't want them to figure out how you did it.

- Borrow objects from the audience. Ask them for coins. Ask them for pencils. This makes tricks seem more real.

- You're going to make mistakes. The audience doesn't know what's happening next. Don't act like you messed up. Just keep going.

- Plan tricks so one trick leads into another. Create a theme. Create a storyline.

- Invite audience members onstage. They like interacting with you.

- Learn some jokes. Make the audience laugh.

- Do not have light behind you. This could give away your trick secrets. It also makes it hard for the audience to see the trick.

Perform an opening trick. There are several tricks you can do for the opener.

This trick is a disappearing coin trick. The audience sees the magician stick a coin into a cloth napkin. The magician turns it over. The coin is gone.

➡ Get a rubber band. Wrap it around your fingers and thumb.

➡ Get a colorful cloth napkin. Place it on top of that hand.

➡ Use your other hand. Place the coin into the napkin.

➡ Let the rubber band slide off of your fingers. The rubber band covers the coin. The coin is under the napkin.

➡ Slide your hand up to the end of the napkin.

➡ Shake it. The coin looks like it disappeared. But it's stuck inside the napkin. It's held by the rubber band.

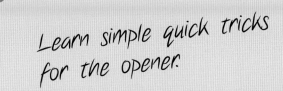

Learn simple quick tricks for the opener.

Perform the middle material trick. There are several tricks you can do. Card tricks are good for middle material. So are prediction tricks. Do a lot of patter.

This is an amazing memory trick. The audience thinks you memorized the order of the cards.

➡ Shuffle the cards.

➡ Make sure the cards are packed together. Quickly look at the bottom card.

➡ Hold the deck behind your back. Tell them the card they'll see.

➡ Take the bottom card. Place it faceup at the top of the deck. Do this behind your back.

➡ Show the deck to the audience. They'll see the old bottom card. Look at the card facing you.

➡ Bring the deck behind your back. Tell them the card they'll see.

➡ **Place the bottom card faceup on top of the deck. Do this behind your back.**

➡ **Show the audience.**

➡ **Repeat steps.**

Don't forget to say magic words.

Perform the closing trick. There are several tricks you can do.

This is a cup levitation trick.

➡ **Get a large, empty paper cup.**

➡ **Make a thumb-size hole in one side of the cup.**

➡ **Hold the empty cup with both of your hands. The hole should be facing you.**

➡ **Tell the audience that you're going to make the cup float.**

➡ **Put your thumb in the hole.**

➡ **Focus on the cup. Stare at it.**

➡ **Open both hands at the same time. Push your hands forward. It looks like you're moving the cup in the air.**

➡ **Slip your thumb out.**

➡ **Let the cup fall.**

Ask guests to fill out feedback forms. Have them write what they liked about your magic show.

There are things you should do at the end of the show.

➡ **Take a bow.**

➡ **Thank the audience for coming.**

➡ **Thank your helpers.**

➡ **Tell the audience to come to your next show!**

D.I.Y. EXAMPLE!

STEPS	EXAMPLES
Type	Street magic
Where	Beach boardwalk
When	Saturday afternoon
Names	Magician Name: The Marvelous Magic-Maker Show Name: Traveling Marvelous Magic Show
Perform opener	◆ Disappearing quarters trick
Perform middle material	◆ Card trick #1 ◆ Memory trick ◆ Card trick #2

STEPS	EXAMPLES
Perform closer	Spoon Bending Trick

- Get a spoon and a coin. Make sure the coin is the same color as the spoon.

- Hide the coin in between your thumb and first finger.

- Use your other hand. Hold the spoon like you're dipping it in a bowl.

- Use the hand with the coin. Put it over the spoon handle. Show a little bit of the coin so that it looks like the end of the spoon handle.

- Bend your hand back and forth. It'll look like the spoon is bending.

- Remove your hands. Let the audience look at the spoon.

- Sneak the coin in your pocket.

GLOSSARY

assistant (uh-SIS-tuhnt) helper

audience (AW-dee-uhns) people who watch a magic show

effects (ih-FEKTS) what people see in magic tricks

escape (ih-SKAPE) getting out of something

illusions (ih-LOO-zhuhnz) magic tricks where people believe they're seeing things that they're not

levitation (lev-ih-TAY-shuhn) making things float

magicians (muh-JISH-uhnz) people who perform magic

mentalism (MEN-tuhl-iz-uhm) reading people's minds

misdirect (mis-dih-REKT) trick or distract

patter (PAT-ur) commentary from a magician while performing tricks

penetration (pen-ih-TRAY-shuhn) passing through something

prediction (prih-DIKT-shuhn) telling what's going to happen next

production (pruh-DUHK-shuhn) producing something from nothing

props (PRAHPS) objects used for tricks

restoration (reh-stor-AY-shuhn) making something come back

sleight of hand (SLITE UHV HAND) hidden movements of the hand

stage magic (STAYJ MAJ-ik) art of entertaining people by performing tricks

stooge (STOOJ) someone who pretends to be an audience member but is really part of the act

transformation (trans-for-MAY-shuhn) changing into something else

transportation (trans-pur-TAY-shuhn) moving things

trunk (TRUHNGK) carrying case

vanish (VAN-ish) make something disappear

INDEX

LEARN MORE

BOOKS

Bree, Loris. *Kids' Magic Secrets: Simple Magic Tricks and Why They Work*. St. Paul, MN: Marlor Press, 2003 and 2007.

Ransford, Sandy. *Master Magician: All You Need to Create Your Own Spectacular Magic Show*. Philadelphia: Running Press Book Publishers, 2002.

WEB SITES

International Magicians Society: www.imsmagic.com

Magic Tricks for Kids: http://magictricksforkids.org

Society of American Magicians: www.magicsam.com